Jolly Roger an

Story by Debbie Croft
Illustrations by Chantal Stewart

Jolly Roger sat on the deck
with his fishing line.
He had one little fish
in his bucket.

"I am **very** hungry today,"
he said.

Then, Jolly Roger got a big fish.

“Now I have a big fish
and a little fish,” he said.

Jolly Roger looked in his bucket.

"Little Pirate," he said.
"Where is my little fish?
Did **you** eat it?"

"No!" said Little Pirate.
"I had lots of berries to eat!"

Jolly Roger sat down again,
but no fish came up to his line.

"I'm **very** hungry," he said.
"I'll have to eat the big fish."

He looked in the bucket,
but the big fish had gone.

"Big Pirate," said Jolly Roger.
"Did **you** eat my big fish?"

"No, not me!" said Big Pirate.
"I had some coconuts!"

"I can see some fish bones,"
said Jolly Roger.

He looked at Little Pirate,
and he looked at Big Pirate.

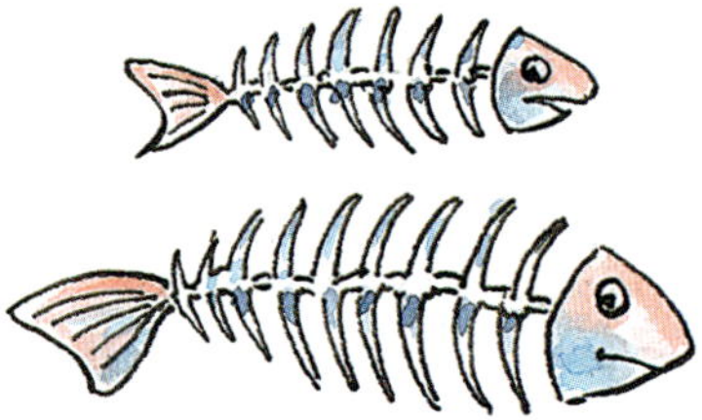

Then, Jolly Roger saw two big eyes!

A black cat ran onto the deck,
and looked into the bucket.

Big Pirate and Little Pirate
laughed and laughed.

Jolly Roger looked at the cat and laughed.

"**You** can't be hungry, now," he said.